Sam Savitt's True Horse Stories

BOOKS BY SAM SAVITT

Step-a-Bit
Midnight
There Was a Horse
Around the World with Horses
Rodeo: Cowboys, Bulls and Broncos
Vicki and the Black Horse
A Day at the L B J Ranch
America's Horses
Equestrian Olympic Sketchbook
Sam Savitt's True Horse Stories

Sam Savitt's True Horse Stories

WRITTEN AND ILLUSTRATED BY SAM SAVITT

Dodd, Mead & Company, New York

Copyright © 1970 by Sam Savitt
All rights reserved
No part of this book may be reproduced in any form
without permission in writing from the publisher
Library of Congress Catalog Card Number: 70-123500
ISBN 0-396-06204-0
Printed in the United States of America

To Bette, Vicki and Roger with Love

Introduction

I have been associating with horses a good part of my life. I have painted horses and written about horses. I've schooled, shown and hunted them. I have studied horses from the saddle looking down and from the ground looking up—after a fall. I have also sat for hours with other horsemen, swapping adventures we've had with these animals, and pored over numerous newspaper and magazine articles concerning horses in history and in sport all over the world.

This book is a roundup of happenings and experiences with horses. I believe they will give you a better understanding of the horse because they are all true.

Contents

Jenny	13	Eclipse	46
The Race	16	Freedom	50
Baily	22	The Phantom Hoofprints	54
The Listening Mare	28	War Bride	60
Lisette—the Female of the Species	32	Pablita	64
		The Story of Sleepy Tom	70
Too Smart	38	The River	76
The Horse They Could Not Forget	42	Midnight	82
		Moifaa	86

Sam Savitt's True Horse Stories

Jenny

THIS happened in upper New York State, around the year 1867, and I'll tell you the story just the way it was told to me.

Dr. Kraft Payson Kimball lived in Burville, a small village just outside of Watertown, New York, but his practice carried him over a good part of the northwest corner of Jefferson County. He made his rounds by horse and buggy, most of the time, but whenever the roads were too muddy or snow covered, he rode a little brown mare named Jenny. The doctor told everyone she had Morgan and Arabian ancestry, but most of all she had a whole lot of good, everyday horse sense.

Now, men who spend many hours on horseback, like cowboys or cavalrymen or country doctors, have learned through necessity the knack of sleeping in the saddle. Doc Kimball was no exception. Many nights, after a long day of house calls, while he slept in the saddle, his good mare Jenny would carry him home. She would plod along quietly, undisturbed by the things that spook most horses, and stop only when she arrived at the doctor's house.

This year the snow had lain deep all winter, and now, in April, with the addition of the constant spring rains, the roads became almost

impassable. Jim McKay, who lived up near Saint Lawrence, had a tree fall on him, and when Jim's boy brought the news, Doc Kimball quickly saddled Jenny and rode out to the McKay place. He set two broken legs and it was well after dark before he was ready to ride for home.

"You can't go out on a night like this, Doc," pleaded Mrs. McKay. "Stay over with us. You can head back in the morning with a good hot breakfast under your belt." But Doc Kimball wouldn't hear of it. He had some pretty sick patients down near Rutland. Besides, the rain had slowed down to a drizzle and he could count on old Jenny to get him back home.

There were twelve miles to go. The doctor settled into the saddle and, with his head tucked into the upturned collar of his oilskin slicker, promptly dozed off.

He didn't know how long he'd slept, but, suddenly, he was startled awake when Jenny came to a halt. He found he was sitting his horse beside the picket fence in front of his own house. The yellow light streaming through the open door, fell across Billy, his stable boy, who was holding Jenny's bridle and peering anxiously up into the doctor's face.

"Are you all right, Doc?" Billy's voice quavered.

"Of course I'm all right—why shouldn't I be?" the doctor answered. He slid to the ground and began unfastening his saddlebag.

"Which way did you come home?"

Billy's question was so intent and irregular that the doctor stopped what he was doing and looked searchingly at the boy.

"The way I always do," he answered softly. "Down Cumberland Road and across Brownville Bridge." He paused to sling the saddlebag across his shoulder.

"Why do you ask, Bill? You know darned well the route I take—it's the only one there is."

"But that's impossible, Doc." Billy's words came slowly and disbelievingly. "Brownville Bridge washed out over four hours ago!"

Next morning Dr. Kimball and Billy went down to the river crossing. Sure enough, the bridge was gone. Only one old rotten beam still spanned the swirling waters. But there in the mud, in the early light, they could see the hoofprints of old Jenny. The doctor and the boy traced them to the crumbling bank and stood in awe and amazement as their eyes unfolded the story of last night.

Old Jenny, in the stormy darkness, with the doctor asleep in the saddle, had crossed that single narrow beam to bring him safely home.

The Race

WHEN we think of horse racing, we are apt to get a picture of high-priced thoroughbreds, immaculately kept stables, immensely wealthy owners, trainers, jockeys and a host of other related matters.

Back in 1875, A. B. Neachan, just finishing a six-year term as Superintendent of Indian Affairs in Oregon, published a now forgotten book, called *Wigwams and Warpath*. In it, I found the following account of another kind of horse race. This one had no grandstand or manicured track and the contestants were no Man O'Wars. The stakes didn't run into the millions of dollars, either, but the tension this race generated was just as unbearable as any emotions roused by the Kentucky Derby, and the results were even more unpredictable.

Haw-lish-wam-po, chief of the Cayuse Indians was the owner of several thousand horses. He was a stoutly built man, past middle-age, but a natural rider and a match for any man in matters pertaining to horses. He also owned a pinto pony who could beat anything in the Umatalla country.

Joe Crab, a white man of questionable character, was also a horseman. He imported from the East a flashy bay thoroughbred for the ex-

press purpose of beating the pinto pony. Some months before, he had surreptitiously watched the pinto run. He had measured the distance, recorded the winner's time, and subsequently tested the speed of his own horse against it. He felt he had a sure thing, and would take the Indian chief for all he was worth.

Crab made known his desire to stage a contest, and the preliminaries were arranged. The race was to be run over the Indian course, located on the bottomlands of the Umatalla River. The turf was smooth and level, and the track was over two and one half miles in length. At the end of the course, a post was planted, around which the racers were to turn and come back to the starting point, making the total distance a little over five and a quarter miles.

But Joe Crab was a greedy and unscrupulous man. He had to be sure. Two nights before the race, he sent a trusted man to get the Indian horse, leaving another in its place. Out on the prairie, he made a few test trials against his own thoroughbred. The result was satisfactory. He found his horse was easily able to outdistance the pinto—so far so good. Barring any unforeseen accident, it would be virtually impossible for him to lose.

When the morning of the race arrived, the roads leading to the valley of the Umatalla gave full proof of the interest the people of the surrounding country had in this important affair. Long before the time of the race, countless carriages, buggies, wagons and horses could be seen assembled along its crest. At the starting point, a great crowd gathered. The Indians were in their galla-day attire—paints, feathers, long hair, red blankets—in fact, it was a dress parade for white and red men alike.

The manner of betting was a far cry from that employed at Churchill Downs. One man was a stakeholder for all the money bets. Horses that were wagered were tied together and put in the care of Indian boys. Other stakes—coats, blankets, saddles, pistols and all kinds of personal effects—were thrown together in a common heap. Two judges were selected, a red man and a white man, one to be stationed at the starting line, the other at the halfway post.

Crab had confided the secret of his stolen trial run to a few friends, advising them to place bets and win all the horses they wanted, since there was no danger of losing. He knew what he was talking about. He

knew the Indian horse's speed by time and trial. This news leaked out. Men who had never bet in their lives became anxious to win a pony or two and laid wagers with the Indians.

Now the two contesting horses were brought out. Crab's imported thoroughbred looked every inch a racer. His whole bearing indicated his superiority. His thin nostrils flared and his neck arched. His coat shone like burnished copper as he pranced restlessly. His jockey, wearing a blue cap, crimson jacket and white breeches, was lifted to the tiny racing saddle. What a picture they made, and what a horrible contrast the little Indian pony offered alongside the bay. He stood unmoved, uncovered, without a saddle, bridle or anything save a small hair rope around his lower jaw. His mane and tail were unkempt, his coat rough and ill-looking. At his right side stood a little Indian boy, with his head close shaven and a blanket wrapped around him. To all appearances, he was unaware that anything unusual was expected. Meanwhile, the other horse was making furious plunges to get away.

The contrast in the spirit and looks of the contending horses was the signal for another charge by Crab's pals on the Indians' betting resources. A few white friends of the Cayuse tribesmen who had heard about Carb's trick came in sympathy to the rescue. But it was too late now. The race was about to begin. Haw-lish-wam-po was calm and undisturbed. He was happy to see the other man's horse shake and fret. The more the better—let him wear himself down. Suddenly, he gave a quiet signal to the Indian rider. The blanket dropped away from the boy's shoulders. He was brown skinned, gaunt-looking, naked to the waist. Like a cat, he vaulted to his pony's back. In his left hand he grasped the hair rope that served as his bridle. In his right was a small bundle of dry willows.

As if by magic, the dull-looking Indian horse became instantly transformed into a beautiful, animated racer. His eyes were on fire. His ears did not droop now, but twitched alertly in quick alternate motions. He was ready. He stamped his feet, slowly at first, but faster and more impatiently as the seconds ticked by. The other horse was making efforts to escape. His rider kept manuvering him for the advantage. Three times the contestants approached the line without managing a start. Crab had become quite pale, perhaps at this moment he sensed that all was not going as planned.

They're off! Both horses sprang into action. Thirty feet from the starting line, the pinto pony was twenty feet in the lead. Away they went and several thousand eyes followed the Indian rider who was still ahead as the horses grew smaller and smaller in the distance. They reached the halfway post and turned for home. It was unbelievable! The Indian pony was still in the lead and really coming on.

Crab seemed to be in shock. "He will win yet," he gasped.

The eagle eyes of Chief Haw-lish-wam-po gleamed as his horse and rider came nearer. The excitement—the screaming and yelling—was beyond description. As they were nearing the starting point, the Indian boy rattled the dry willows over his pony, who, considering the nature of the turf, was making the fastest time on record. The Indians along the line fell in and ran beside the victorious racer, encouraging him with wild shouts while he crossed the finish line in an unprecedented time of nine minutes and fifty-one seconds.

After the tumult had died down and all the bets had been paid off,

THE RACE

Haw-lish-wam-po gave back to Crab the saddle horse he had won from him and money to travel on. He did not let the stunned man know that he had arranged for his pinto to be purposely held back when Crab had checked his time. He also did not tell his opponent that he had secretly substituted the pinto's half brother to be used for that test run on the prairie. The chief had foreseen this clandestine move and had put his racing pony in safe seclusion that night.

But what he did say to Crab was, "My friend, when you steal a competitor's horse to race him alone—be sure you know how to make him run!"

Baily

BAILY was among the most talented but also the most exasperating of all the horses I have ever owned. I first saw him at a riding clinic where riders and horses get together for work and instruction on the finer points of horsemanship. During the entire class, I couldn't get my eyes off this spirited bay horse. He was a close coupled thoroughbred with a broad white blaze down the middle of his face. One eye had a little too much white and he was a bit Roman nosed, but what caught my interest was the way he moved—rythmically and beautifully balanced like a boxer. He was being ridden badly by a young man, but, despite his rider, he showed more than an adequate amount of ability and, even though he was acting like an idiot most of the time, I felt this display didn't really belong to him—that underneath it all was one mighty fine horse and I wanted him. If I had known then what I was letting myself in for, I would have backed off and let the whole thing drop. Instead, I negotiated with his owner for several weeks, then, one day around the middle of March, I bought him.

Baily had the makings of a terrific hunter, and he proved to be one of the finest jumpers I ever took over a stone wall, or a coop, or a post

and rail, or any other kind of fence that crisscrossed our countryside. He was a natural, and I felt that, with the education I could give him, there was no telling how far he could go.

Of course, he had his problems and I methodically set to work straightening them out. For instance, when I slipped a bridle over his ears, just as the bit was going into his mouth, Baily would snap his head to the left with such force that there were times when I was knocked clean across the stall. My first instinct was to strike back, but this would be exactly the wrong thing to do. I once heard a baby doctor say, referring to children, "At the times when they are the least lovable, they need the most love." This without a doubt held true, especially for Baily. He had been roughed up before. This offense was his defense and because, by nature, he was an aggressive character, he struck out first, in anticipation of what he expected. But I didn't strike back. I worked patiently and quietly and after several weeks, he was bridled with no difficulty.

Over a jump, he would snap his head up, this time anticipating being jerked in the mouth by hands that had been too hard and unrelenting. I worked him over fences on a loose rein until he realized that jumping could be as pleasant an experience as cantering across a grassy field. Little by little, he learned that the things I asked of him were not unreasonable and always painless. His progress was most rewarding. Before I bought him, he was hacked along the roads in a strong Kimberwick bit which bruised his tender mouth. Now, I could hunt him behind hounds in a light snaffle bit and one couldn't find a better mannered horse anywhere.

His stablemate was my wife's hunter, Pat, and in no time at all, Baily was deeply attached to him. Horses are, by nature, gregarious creatures and usually form strong attachments to their buddies. But not the way Baily did. With him, it was not an attachment, but an obsession. He simply could not bear to be separated from Pat. Yet, in a way, he was strangely inconsistent. I frequently exercised both horses. Baily left the barn with no fuss and went straight to work. But when I took Pat out and left Baily in he became a completely different animal. I could hear his wild banshee cries as I trotted Pat away from the barn— and they did not cease. Off in the fields, his voice still persisted and as Pat and I approached the barn coming home, it grew louder and more hysterical. I was appalled by the sight of his stall, all churned up, with more holes in the stall floor than there are in a hunk of Swiss cheese. But more exasperating was the inevitable fact that, even though I had been riding Pat, it was the dripping wet Baily I had to walk for twenty minutes until he cooled out. It was a ridiculous situation and nothing I tried seemed to help cure it.

Once, after I had left the barn with Pat, my wife, Bette, turned Baily out in the pasture, thinking perhaps he would look around, knicker once or twice, then take to grazing as any sensible horse would. However, Baily galloped back and forth along the fence line until his sides were lathered and heaving so hard you'd think he had just run in the Grand National.

In the hunting field, Bette on Pat had to stay behind us. If they moved on ahead, Baily plunged about like a green colt, then lugged into the bit, trying to catch up. When hounds are running, and sixty horses are out there, galloping on, that sort of nonsense can be disastrous.

But this was only a small part of Baily's shenanigans. In all the years I have had horses, I have always found my pasture fencing to be more than adequate. But Baily quickly demolished my complacent attitude. This horse could untie any knot or open any gate on the place. It was amusing to watch him size up a barway. First he would clamp his teeth on the top tail, to see if it would lift. Then he'd slide it from side to side. Next, he'd snake his head under and try lifting it. If that didn't work, he would step back and study the situation, then try another approach. The truth of the matter was that Baily was too smart. Fortunately, under saddle, he was most cooperative, but left to his own devices, he became a scheming devil and what I found to be amusing in the beginning grew to be about as pleasurable as a horseshoe in my pants pocket.

I was forced to re-do all my fencing. I found that snap catches were the only things Baily could not open—and these, with short chains and screw eyes, soon decorated every gate and barway he could reach. He would also slide the bolt of his stall door, then open Pat's and together they would romp over the countryside, sometimes getting me up in the middle of the night to give chase and catch Baily before he could turn loose the cattle in the farmyard across the road.

I built a shelf over the bolt of his stall door, to keep him from getting at it, and another shelf over the water faucet after he turned it on one night and flooded the barn. I had light switches installed when I found he was turning the lights on by pulling the cords—then later, had to box in the switches when he learned he could accomplish the same thing with them. It was absolutely crazy. I was getting punchy—for now, instead of working at my painting, drawing and writing, I found myself sitting in my studio devising Rube Goldberg contraptions in a vain and hopeless effort to outsmart this maddening horse. Finally, I decided that, despite all his talent and ability, Baily had to go.

A wealthy young man, who fox hunted with Bette and me, bought him. He had been looking for a young thoroughbred who would hunt

on a snaffle and jump any fence in our countryside. This kind was hard to come by, but Baily filled the bill without question.

I trailered him to his new home. The stable was like something out of *House & Gardens,* roomy, immaculately kept, deep straw bedding —but, most important of all, the convivial bay would have twenty-seven show and race horses for company.

Baily, you've got it made, I thought to myself. You will never be left alone again.

All was peaceful and Baily seemed quite relaxed. I told the manager he would probably miss Pat for a day or two, but get over it. The manager agreed. An exercise boy came in, opened the stall door next to Baily and led its occupant out. As they walked down the alleyway to the outside doorway, Baily blew his stack. His screams of anguish split the stillness with such impact, the other horses in the stable took to whinnying and plunging about. The battle was on. Suddenly, I knew what I hadn't realized until this moment. It wasn't Pat that Baily missed—not at all! It was any horse next door. For Baily was the equine version of "When I'm not near the girl I love, I love the girl I'm near."

As the weeks went by, the situation worsened. The tranquility of Baily's new home was shattered and when I heard about it, I told Bette that, if that vocalizing animal didn't learn to keep his big mouth shut, sure as shootin', somebody was going to shut it for good. I had felt like it many times. The stable manager tried to solve this predicament by switching Baily's stall periodically, in an effort to break up his pattern of association and uncompromising devotion to the horse in the next stall.

But Baily's cries could not be stilled. His new owner would have gotten rid of him in a moment, but, as he told me afterwards, "Baily is the best hunter I have ever owned. There must be a way!" And there was.

This clever fellow bought Baily a roommate of his own, a donkey who never left his side. When the horse got in from hunting, his little companion was always there to greet him and when he was turned out in the pasture, his friend went with him.

I suppose Baily, in his horsey way, yearned for someone he could call his own, and when he finally found him, he was content.

The Listening Mare

NOT too long ago, while I was researching material on the Arabian Horse, I came across an unusual story about the Kehilan Al Maisan or Listening Horses, a line of Arabians especially valued for their intelligence, beauty and endurance. This is how they acquired that strange designation.

At the end of a long day's march, after a foray on a neighboring tribe, a band of the warlike Anazeh pitched camp for the night. One of the sheiks unsaddled his mare and turned her out with her foal. All the horses and men were tired and hungry, but instead of feeding, the mare stood, her head high, with every appearance of intently listening. Her dark eyes seemed to be fixed on some distant point beyond the horizon, with her flaring nostrils quivering as they searched the whispering wind.

The other sheiks and members of the tribe gathered around to observe the strange behavior of the mare. They tried putting a nosebag of barley on her head. In the midst of munching the grain, her jaws would stop, up would go her head and the attitude of motionless listening would be resumed.

Her owner removed her hobbles and turned her loose. She ran

around in circles, ignoring her foal, but eventually would come back to the same listening posture, facing in the same direction. Nothing could distract her. It was as if something out there in the night had an invisible hold on her. Her master had never seen her so disturbed. When he placed a quieting hand against her long arched neck, she paid him no heed, but he felt a dampness of her skin and a strange tenseness throbbing beneath it.

THE LISTENING MARE

He turned to the other tribesmen and cried, "My mare senses danger. She is trying to tell me an enemy is approaching. We must saddle up and move out before it is too late!"

His companions all refused to take his warning seriously, for that would be carrying things too far. They were very tired and, after all, she was only a horse, wasn't she?

Perhaps she was, but regardless, her owner hurriedly folded his tents, mounted his mare and fled the camp with his family and retainers. The ridicule of his fellow tribesmen followed his flight.

That night there occurred one of the greatest massacres in the history of the Anazeh Bedouins. Shortly before dawn, the enemy swept down on the sleeping camp . . . When the sun arose, the wind still blew softly across the shifting sands, but now vultures circled against the brightening sky.

Many miles to the south, the fleeing sheik pulled up to water and feed his tired mare. She had warned her master and carried him to safety. Forever after, her descendants would carry the name Kehilan Al Maisan—Listening Horses.

Lisette — the Female of the Species

"THE female of the species is deadlier than the male." This old adage may apply to cats or wolves, or numerous other predatory animals, but never to a horse who is basically a creature of flight not fight. Eddie Arcaro, the great jockey, once said, "The one thing I know for sure about a horse is that you never know!" Here is a true story about a horse who lived up to both of these quotations.

Baron de Marbot was an officer in the French army during the Napoleonic wars. He was in the market for a cavalry mount when he learned that a Mr. Finguerlin, a wealthy horse breeder, had a beautiful chestnut mare for sale. She was called Lisette, and when the Baron rode her he found her gaits most comfortable, she moved lightly as a deer. And under saddle her manners were beyond reproach.

"She can be led about by a child," her owner informed him. "But there is one terrible fault—she bites like a bulldog and will furiously attack anybody she dislikes."

This statement would have fixed me. I wouldn't have that kind of a horse as a gift. But the Baron bought her for one thousand francs. In that respect he was getting a bargain because she had cost Mr. Finguerlin five thousand francs.

Needless to say, she was a terror from the moment she arrived at the Baron's stable. First she gave him an ugly bite on the shoulder and, within two days, she had bitten several other people on the place. After two weeks and several more narrow escapes, the Baron decided to get rid of her. He had meanwhile engaged a new stable manager named Francis Woirland, who was afraid of nothing—no female horse was going to push him around! Armed with a good hot roast leg of mutton, he went out to meet Lisette. She immediately lunged at him, but instead of his arm, she got a mouthful of burning hot mutton. With a scream of pain, she let go, but not before she was severely burned on her tongue and gums. From that moment, she was perfectly submissive to Woirland and didn't try to attack him again. The Baron used the same method with like results and, in a very short time, he and his manager were perfectly safe in her company. In a little while, she even became more tractable to the stablemen on the staff—but woe to the stranger who passed near her!

Not long after her arrival, one of the servants reported that sacks of grain were being stolen from the stable. That night, Lisette was left loose near the door. In the dark hour before dawn an unearthly shriek errupted from the stable area. The thief was carrying off a sack of grain when the mare seized him by the neck and, screaming in agony, he was dragged out into the paddock. Before the man could be rescued, he was trampled severely and suffered two broken ribs. Lisette was the mare that carried the Baron de Marbot into war. This account, from his memoirs, is what took place there.

"We were engaged in the battle of Eylou. Our corps under General Augereau was trying to rally near the great cemetery. The fourteenth of the line had remained alone on a hillock which it could not quit except by the Emporer's order. The snow had ceased for a moment and from where we were massed, we could see this regiment surrounded by the enemy, waving its eagle in the air to ask for support.

"At the last moment, the Emporer decided to try to save these brave men and instructed Augereau to send an officer to them with

LISETTE — THE FEMALE OF THE SPECIES

orders to abandon the hill, form a small square and make their way toward us, while a brigade of cavalry should march out to assist their withdrawal.

"There was a swarm of Cossacks between us and the fourteenth and it was clear that any officer that was sent toward the unfortunate regiment would be killed or captured before he got there.

"Two went before me. They rode out with swords drawn and were shot down before they were halfway there.

"When I was called, I decided that to try to cut my way through would be ill considered. The only way possible was to go at it as if I were riding in a steeplechase—straight to the appointed goal, the fourteenth, and to look neither to right or left and completely disregard the Cossacks.

"This plan worked perfectly. Lisette, lighter than a swallow and flying rather than running, devoured the intervening space, leaping the piles of dead men and horses and ditches and broken gun carriages. Thousands of Cossacks swarmed over the plain. The first who saw me acted like sportsmen who had flushed a hare and kept shouting to their comrades further up the line, 'You take him! You take him!'

"But none of them tried to stop me. This was probably due to my extremely rapid pace, but also because each thought I could not avoid the others further on. I escaped them all and Lisette and I reached the fourteenth without a scratch.

"I found the remnants of this regiment formed in a square on the top of the hill. Great billows of smoke rose around them. All about was the din of musket fire and the shrieks and snaps of ricocheting bullets. Their Commander cried, 'I see no way of saving the regiment. Bid the Emporer farewell from the fourteenth of the line and give him the eagle which we can defend no longer!' Meanwhile, the column of Russian Grenadiers hurled themselves furiously on the feeble remains of this regiment. The noise was deafening. Lisette was steady under me, but all about us was the clash and slash of steel and the agonizing screams of the wounded. It was at this moment that a grenadier drove his bayonette into my mare's thigh.

"Since she had entered the army, Lisette had become the model of good behavior, but when that bayonette cut into her flesh, all her savage instincts leaped back to the surface again. Her ears flattened so close to

her head, she resembled a serpent and with a shriek of pain, she sprang at the Russian. In one horrible bite she tore off the man's face, leaving only a bloody death's head. Then like a tigress, she hurled herself at the grenadiers, kicking, slashing, ripping her way into the struggling men. A Cossack caught hold of her bridle. She seized him by the belly and jerked him from the saddle, smashed him into the ground and tore him wide open with her hoofs and left him dying in the snow. Then taking the road by which she had come, she made her way at full gallop back towards the cemetery at Eylau. At this point, I was hanging onto my Hussar's saddle for dear life.

"But a new danger awaited. As I approached my own regiment, because of the falling snow, the battalion of the old guard mistook me for an enemy officer leading a charge. The whole battalion opened fire at once. My cloak and my saddle were riddled. But Lisette and I were untouched. Three ranks of battalion were in front of us but we went through them like a snake through a hedge. This last spurt had exhausted my mare's strength. She had lost much blood and as she galloped on, suddenly her legs gave way and she went down, pinning me beneath her.

"Stretched on the snow, among the piles of dead and dying, unable to move, I felt that the end was near. Gradually, and without pain, I lost consciousness and became oblivious to the mighty clatter of Murat's ninety cavalry squadrons which passed over me advancing to the charge."

LISETTE — THE FEMALE OF THE SPECIES

The Baron de Marbot and Lisette lay out there in the snow-covered battlefield all day. Around sundown, he was rescued by an old friend from the rear area. Meanwhile, gangrene had set into an old wound in his frozen foot. But the doctors and four servants cut out the damaged part and dripped hot sweetened wine into the wound for eight days to save his foot from amputation. They tied the Baron upright in a carriage body on a sled, which required from twelve to sixteen horses to draw it at a walk along the muddy roads of Siberia and on to France.

How did the mare make out? Well, you've also heard the saying, "The good die young." Lisette followed this adage to the letter, so she had nothing to worry about. The intense February cold of two degrees had clotted the blood in her wound and both horse and man recovered completely, to fight together again in June, at nearby Friedland.

Too Smart

*J*UST how intelligent are thoroughbreds? It seems that almost every trainer has a favorite story that portrays the intelligence of a particular thoroughbred that he had contact with at one time or another. Elsewhere in this book, I have told you the story of my thoroughbred, Baily, who was too smart. But even though he was bad news in the stable, under saddle, he was a terrific performer. Now, I am going to tell you of another kind of rogue and you can decide how smart this one really was.

R. V. Johnson was a race-horse trainer who practiced in the State of California and the horse this story is about was a three-year-old chestnut thoroughbred named Who Know. The colt had an obvious calcium deposit in his knee, but it appeared to be an old injury and he was winning races.

One afternoon, as Johnson was cooling him out after a race, he noticed that the horse "nodded" just a little as he walked, but he didn't appear to be too sore. This was not unusual. The trainer figured that, with a good rubdown, the colt would sleep the strain off and, sure enough, during the next morning's walk, there was no sign of lameness.

His knee was cool and it seemed that the sweat lotion Johnson had applied the night before had drawn out any soreness that might have been present.

He gave Who Know a three-day layoff, then, on the fourth day, decided it was time to put him back to work. The groom brought the horse out and held him as Johnson threw on the tack. Joe Michaelson, the exercise boy, got a leg up and while he perched there, adjusting his irons, Johnson gave him instructions for the morning workout.

As the horse and jockey moved off toward the track, Johnson's mouth dropped open in dismay. Who Know was dead lame, so lame he could barely touch his toe to the ground! Johnson was completely bewildered. "I don't understand it, Joe. I'd swear this horse was as sound as a ten-dollar gold piece just a minute ago—right now, he's so touchy he can barely walk, let alone gallop."

TOO SMART

He unsaddled the horse and put him back in his stall. It was a puzzling situation, but what mystified him more was the fact that there was no apparent heat in the knee.

The next morning, the colt again walked out without any sign of lameness. The way he kicked up his heels and played during his walk decided Johnson that Who Know was well enough to spend his energy in a good gallop. But the moment the saddle was on his back, Who Know started to limp.

This routine was repeated several times during the next few days and it became obvious that the horse was an accomplished faker. Just show him a saddle and he'd go into his act. Evidently, the colt was lazy and didn't like to be exercised. Somewhere along the way, he had learned that if he acted lame, he wouldn't have to work.

Who Know's faking finished him in the racing field, though, for how could Johnson explain to a track veterinarian who was putting the horse on the vet's list for being lame that the animal was only faking?

You might exclaim here, "Well, that son of a gun really got away with it." He didn't. Who Know was sold and for almost a year drifted from one riding academy to another. However, most riding schools cannot afford to support an animal who does not do his share of work. The A. S. P. C. A. would never tolerate using a lame one. So eventually, because of his "chronic lameness" the horse was destroyed.

Now there are those who might say Who Know was too smart for his own good—but I think he wasn't smart enough.

The Horse They Could Not Forget

NEAR Fort Snelling, in Minnesota, on a grassy knoll, there is a tombstone which reads:

> WHISKEY
> A Great Horse
> A Stout Heart
> 1911—1943

Any time you see it, rain or shine, winter or summer, there are always flowers decorating its base. True, they are artificial, but they are always there. And as you look down at the gray stone, you wonder, who was Whiskey and who is it that loved this horse so much that, to his dying day, he will put flowers on this grave?

Well, let me tell you about this horse. He came to Fort Snelling from Montana in 1921, with a consignment of remounts for the Army.

His service record showed that he was foaled in 1911 and, upon arrival at the post, weighed 950 pounds, stood 15.1 hands in height. He soon earned a reputation as an outlaw and was named Whiskey because of his drunkenlike antics when anyone tried to ride him. He would have been given a fast dishonorable discharge but for Lieutenant William R. Hazelrigg, a Kentuckian, who recognized in Whiskey the makings of a fine mount and, under his training the rebel became one of the most famous jumping and trick horses the United States has ever produced.

He demonstrated his prowess at military functions, at fairs, and many other exhibitions. His pictures appeared in the rotogravure sections of the largest newspapers, from New York to San Francisco. His repertoire included, among many other skills, jumping over a span of mules, diving through flaming hoops and playing dead.

After performing for many years, he was retired to pasture on August 10, 1936, by order of Brigadier General David L. Stone, Commander of Fort Snelling at this time.

But Whiskey was not through yet. By special permission of the Secretary of War, he was permitted to perform at the St. Paul Winter Carnival in February 1939, under the watchful eyes of his caretaker, Sergeant W. E. Johnson, 3rd Infantry. After a stellar performance, he went back to his hay and oats, furnished by the Army. When World War II broke, the Army became completely mechanized. Tanks, motorcycles and jeeps took over and there was scant time or money for a useless horse.

Now Whiskey came out of retirement to earn his own keep. In 1941, over one thousand people watched him star at a benefit program to collect money for his own sustenance.

A reporter on the St. Paul Dispatch wrote: "The crowd cheered. The band played. Whiskey's head went up. He turned toward the band. He lifted a foot—his tail twitched. The audience was with him. He was an actor again, with poise and confidence. Guided by his trainer, Sergeant Hurley Evans, he took sugar from the Sergeant's mouth and thanked him with a kiss. He played dead on a pile of hay and as a grand climax, he jumped over a flaming bar, hung between flaming posts.

The war rolled on. In September 1943, the man who first recognized Whiskey's potential, now Colonel William R. Hazelrigg, went six hundred miles out of his way to visit his friend, who he hadn't seen in seventeen years. The old horse recognized him from afar and came running to nuzzle the man he had never forgotten.

Shortly after, in December 1943, Whiskey died and was buried with full military honors. Perhaps the days of the horse cavalry are gone forever but the memory of this horse is not dead. For, of those who saw him or handled him, there is one who still puts flowers on Whiskey's grave.

Eclipse

MOST people who are asked, "Who was one of the greatest race horses in history?" usually answer automatically, "Man O'War." Man O'War was indeed one of the all-time greats. But the most famous race horse was Eclipse, so named because he was foaled in England during an eclipse of the sun, in 1764.

The colt, who stood 15.2 hands, was not much for looks, but he had a proud heritage which traced back directly to the Darley Arabian, one of the three founding sires of the thoroughbred race horse.

Eclipse was bred by the Duke of Cumberland, and, when still a yearling, he was sold for the equivalent of $400. to William Wildman, a prosperous meat salesman with an intense interest in horse racing.

The colt early manifested such a nasty disposition it seemed probable that he would have to be gelded. This kind of temperament indicated an aggressive side to his nature which is, actually, a most important ingredient in the make-up of a top race horse. I know several breeders who turn out all their young stock together. Many of the animals get bitten and kicked, but the owners find that the most aggressive ones make the best runners.

Wildman refused to curb his horse's fiery spirit by gelding. Instead, he put Eclipse in the hands of a notoriously rough rider who worked the thoroughbred day and night. Even this rigorous treatment had little effect on his mean disposition. But Eclipse ran like the wind and, the harder he ran, the more the frisky colt enjoyed himself.

Before 1776, because of the gruelling four-mile heat system of racing, horses did not run until they had reached the age of five. This made sense, especially when you consider that a horse does not reach maturity until that time. And this system, which required three four-mile heats under saddle in a single afternoon, would be much too hard on a younger animal. Today, horses begin racing at two, so it is easy to understand why so many are broken-down wrecks before they've had a chance to grow up.

Eclipse arrived at the age of five and started in his first race at Epsom Downs on May 3, 1769. One of the bettors, a wealthy Irishman named Dennis O'Kelly, who had made a fortune gambling, watched the blazed-face chestnut win the first heat easily. He was so impressed with Eclipse's performance that he shrewdly bet he could name the order in which each horse in the race would finish. Asked for his wager, he cried prophetically, "Eclipse first, the rest nowhere." The prediction was correct and the phrase became famous. After Eclipse had repeated his superb performance in his second race at Ascot, O'Kelly persuaded Wildman to sell him a half interest in the horse for about $3,250. By 1770, Wildman had foolishly signed away his remaining half interest

ECLIPSE

to O'Kelly for $5,500. So a horse who was responsible, directly or through his get, for hundreds of millions of dollars changing hands, was snapped up for a few thousand dollars by a gambler with vision.

Eclipse raced only three seasons, winning all his twenty-six starts and eleven King's plates. For ten of the races he carried the unusually heavy load of 168 pounds. He was never defeated or even extended, and he beat by at least two hundred yards the best horses in England. In October 1771, he raced for the last time as a seven-year-old at New Market. After that, O'Kelly retired Eclipse to stud and English racing again became a competitive contest.

Eclipse was so famous in his day that the average Britisher knew him as well as the King himself. His portrait was painted at least a dozen times and one horse lover, Lord Roseberry, owned eight portraits of him well over a hundred years after the horse's death. Even the British Museum displayed an engraving of him on its sacrosanct walls. He died at the age of twenty-five, in 1789, and the public scrambled to own and marvel at his remains. His skeleton was mounted and earnestly studied by scientists who wrote profound treatises explaining the horse's exceptional ability to run. His heart was carefully weighed and found to be five pounds heavier than that of the average horse. His mane and tail were woven into a racing trophy (the New Market Challenge Whip), and one mounted hoof was acquired by royalty. The interest in the relics of Eclipse was so great that a brisk business sprang up in ersatz remains of the horse. At least six "undoubted" skeletons and nine "authentic" feet were foisted on a gullible souvenir seeking public. Dennis O'Kelly would have gotten a real kick out of such daring business enterprise—but he had died of the gout the year before the demise of his horse.

Today, the legendary Eclipse is as well known as he was when O'Kelly owned him. He is remembered not only for his incomparable racing but for the number of worthy descendents he left to the turf world. Gallant Fox, Whirlaway, Assault, Citation, Nashua, Swaps, are among those familiar to American horse lovers.

Eclipse's blood, transmitted through his famous sons, has proved to be the most valuable of any horse on record. Man O'War was one of the greatest race horses of our time, but the fractious chestnut colt, Eclipse, born over two hundred years ago, eclipsed them all.

Freedom

TODAY, almost any time you pick up a newspaper or listen to a news broadcast you learn about a country or an individual or a group, somewhere in this world, that is battling for freedom. I realize this fight has been going on since the beginning of time and probably always will be waged. But whenever I consider this everlasting conflict, it invariably brings to my mind the true story of a horse, a wild mustang stallion, who also believed in freedom. They called him Starface. He was a deep bay, with a white star-shaped patch on his forehead and a stocking on his right forefoot. In 1878, he was commanding a large band of mustangs that ranged between the Cimmeron and Curumpa Rivers, in No Man's Land—the westward-pointing panhandle of Oklahoma. He was the boldest, most gallant and the most magnificent thief the Cimmeron ranges had ever known.

Many ranchmen in No Man's Land had horse herds as well as cattle and some raised only horses. Whenever Starface felt the blood stir in him, he would raid down upon these ranch horses, fight off the domestic stallions, cut out a bunch of mares, with or without foals, and herd them back into his own well-trained bunch.

The harassed ranchers organized to capture him. They took hundreds of long distance shots at him, they cut off most of his followers, but he still ran free. Finally, in desperation, they picked four cowboys, furnished them with the strongest and fastest horses in the country and told them not to come back until they had killed or captured Starface.

The four scouted for nearly a week before they sighted the stallion's band. By keeping out of sight and riding in relays, they dogged the suspicious mustang for three days and nights. They studied the habits and routines of these wild horses and marveled at the discipline by which the bay controlled his band. Now he would leave them and graze off alone, and not a mare would dare follow. At times, he would round them into a tight knot from which no yearling would dare break. Again, he would move out with every animal obediently at his heels.

It was early fall and the moon was in full quarter. Just past midnight on the fourth night, the two cowboys on watch saw Starface leave his band and head all alone for the river flats. One man followed while his companion sped back to arouse the others. For six miles the stallion galloped into the north, and so intent was he on his quest that he never looked back.

Presently, he swung right to enter a grassy canyon which spread out between walls of rock. Not far above the brink of the canyon, Starface passed through a narrow gateway of boulders shutting in a small valley. Shortly before dawn, the cowboys came to the pass. They knew the boxed structure of this canyon and were certain that, before long, the bay stallion would be coming back this way with his newly stolen mares. They decided to wait. By now, all four were determined to catch Starface rather than kill him, for studying him at close hand had changed their vengeance into admiration. In the early light of morning, they watched the bold stallion returning with about a dozen mares and foals. He was intent on the business of keeping them grouped, and, for once, he was off guard. He had worked the mares into the pass where the walls were about a hundred feet apart when, suddenly, the four mounted riders leaped from behind the boulders and came pounding down. Their wild Texas yells, punctuated by the blast of their 45's, blew the stallion's band wide apart.

Quick as a cat, Starface wheeled and charged alone up the steep canyon side. As he ascended, the sun's rays, breaking over the rim of the

FREEDOM

wall on the opposite side of the canyon, caught the shimmering gleam of his muscles while he struggled upward. Now the cowboys were three jumps behind. They saw the stallion leap to a bench as wide perhaps as a corral. Towering above that bench was the caprock, without a seam or slope in its face. Starface had picked the only spot at which the bench could be gained. But, unlike the canyon floor from which he had fled, it ended in space—a sheer drop of ninety feet to the Cimmaron. It had rained heavily upcountry, and the white water below was raging and twisting its way between the many crags and boulders.

"Come on, we've got him!" yelled one of the mustangers. He uncoiled his rope as his mount lunged up the way which the mustang had just ascended.

Who knows what desperate motivation urged on this freedom-loving horse at that moment. He must have realized his capture was imminent but, because he was a creature of flight, he made the only choice his wild unrestrained nature would permit. At the brink of the shelf, he gathered his feet as if to vault the Cimmeron itself, and then, without hesitating one second, he sprang into space. With mane and tail streaming defiantly out behind, he plunged downward. He struck the water like a bullet, and instantly disappeared in the foaming roar of the river.

The first cowboy gained the bench. He slid from his saddle and threw himself flat at the edge of the cliff. Far below, he saw Starface surface and swim strongly with the current, making for the opposite shore. The river carried him around the bend and he was lost from sight.

The cowboy rose wearily to his feet and walked back to his blowing horse. He loosened the girth to let the animal breathe easier. The other three men arrived and dismounted. Nobody said a word but in their hearts was a happiness they could not explain.

Starface was never seen again in the Cimmeron Country, and I suppose no one will ever know for sure what happened to him. I think that somewhere, away from man, he made a fresh start and found a new life.

The Phantom Hoofprints

TODAY, with the tremendous advances in science and the exploration of space, it becomes increasingly impossible to disbelieve anything, no matter how fantastic it may seem. Here is a story of a horse and a man, a legend so to speak, that has survived for more than a hundred and fifty years. To this very day, the hoofprints which climax this incident can be seen. Every year, thousands of motorists view these phantom prints which are located about two hundred yards from North Carolina highway 92, between Washington, North Carolina, and Bath.

As the legend goes, a man named Elliot owned a silver-white stallion whom he considered to be the fastest thing on four legs. Elliot, a foul-mouthed individual, was the leader of a pleasure-loving group of the neighborhood. They were a rough and ready bunch. Every Sunday, they drank and gambled and raced their horses, with no regard for the Sabbath observance in the little settlement.

On this particular Sunday in early spring, the group was gathered in a grove at the far end of the county. They had been drinking heavily all afternoon. The men were sprawled on the ground amidst the debris of empty beer kegs while neighborhood dogs nosed about in the grass

for bits of discarded bread and meat. The horses were grazing nearby. Their saddles were still on, but the bridles had been taken off. They moved about in a roped-in grassy enclosure, with swarms of sparrows darting in and out between their feet. It was a most peaceful scene. The white stallion was standing apart from the others. His head was up, for he was watching his master, who was hunched back against a tree, eyeing his horse.

"Yes, sir," he mumbled, "that damn horse of mine can beat anything in the country. Show him to me and we'll take him!"

He lurched to his feet and stared belligerently at his inebriated friends, lying about.

"I tell you," he roared, "my horse can beat any nag around here." He rocked forward. "Anyone want to bet?"

Ernie Mulligan, small and wiry, woke up in time to hear the challenge. "I'll take you up on that. Your dairy herd against mine." He paused before he added, "But it's got to be a distance race—your horse might be a sprinter, but mine's got the stamina."

"The hell he has!" Elliot shot back.

Johannas Green cut in, "When it comes to stamina and distance, my Tommy Boy can take you both—especially on Sunday."

They all guffawed and began placing their bets.

The distance was to be eight miles, over the road running due north between Bath and Blakesly Junction. Mike Frazier rode on ahead, to be at the finish line, where the old Methodist Church stood, at the south edge of Bath.

Elliot staggered over to his horse. He shoved the bridle up over his ears and jammed the steel bit against the stallion's teeth.

"Open up there!" He belched. "We've got a race to win."

The horse was used to this kind of rough treatment—and he always took it without flinching. There was a proud, disdainful look in his eyes, which constantly irritated Elliot. Sometimes it made him so angry that he'd back the horse into a corner of his stall and lay it on him with a chain. But he was never able to break that defiant nature. Some used to wonder why the horse would run and win for him, but others prophesied, "That old horse is just biding his time—one of these days you wait and see."

Today, Elliot swung up into the saddle and jerked the stallion's

head around toward the starting line. The two other contestants were already there, waiting to begin. Their horses, both bays, were stamping nervously, but when the white stallion joined them they became quiet. It hardly seemed as if a race was about to begin. Off in the thickets, the crickets stopped chirping. The white stallion flexed his powerful neck and snorted. Miller Kent stood swaying beside the racers. He raised his right hand aloft.

"One, two,—Go!" he roared.

The three horses lunged forward as one, not because their riders were alert and ready, which they were not, but because the horses were. They had raced often, and the word "Go," shouted this way, meant just what it said.

Down the old country road they went. The sun had set and, in the afterglow of twilight, the white stallion glowed florescent as he shot by his rivals. Elliot was hunched forward, his arms flopping with every stride and his black coattails whipping out behind. After the first turn, he had left the two others in a swirl of choking dust . . . about four miles up the road, the pair began catching up. Elliot could hear the rhythmic snort of their mounts' breathing. The trees and countryside were blurring past, but the staccato drum of the flying hoofs drew nearer and nearer.

Elliot heard Green shout, "Come on, Tommy Boy, let's take 'em." Glancing back over his shoulder, he could see the dark horse pulling alongside. He was frantic. His throat was on fire. His whip rose and fell in loud snapping cracks. Up ahead, he could see the Methodist Church looming white against the darkening landscape. He screamed into his horse's ear, "Get me there first, you white son of Satan, or take me to hell!"

Suddenly, a thing happened which the others present would remember to their dying day. No sooner were these words out of Elliot's mouth, when the white stallion faltered in his stride. Then, as if he were propelled by some giant force, he leaped ahead in two great bounds—and came to a jarring halt, six feet in front of a magnificent old oak. Elliot shot out of the saddle and crashed into the tree trunk.

The other two men stopped their horses as soon as they could. All their drunkenness had vanished. They turned back and, as they approached the tree, they could see Elliot lying there, flat on his back. Death had met him head-on, face to face, and with such force and unexpectancy that the man's mouth was agape and the eyes were wide open, glassy, terrified, as if they had just seen the devil himself.

The white stallion was nowhere to be found and, what's more, he was never seen again. For days, the countryside was searched for miles around, but the horse seemed to have vanished from the earth.

The spectacular circumstance of Elliot's death made a deep impression on the residents of the province, especially when, shortly thereafter, the magnificent tree, against which the rider had been hurled, died, while the deep holes dug by the stallion's hoofs remained.

The depressions are still there. Eight pits, spaced to fit the idea that they were made by two sudden jumps of the white horse, have been on the land of Ed Cutler ever since his family has had the farm, which is nearly a century. Every man in the neighborhood remembers how, as a child, he tried to fill those pits and how, a few days later, they always

THE PHANTOM HOOFPRINTS

appeared exactly as they were before. And each man remembers that his father, as a child, did the same thing.

Many years ago, the land was given over to pigs who trampled the ground into mud, but the tramplings never succeeded in erasing the hoofprints. Rain fails to cover or deepen them, and dry weather finds them hard and packed. Sticks and stones put over them mysteriously disappear. Scientists hazard the theory that the depressions might be caused by underground warm air pockets—but to the people of Bath, they remain a providential warning: "Hoofprints of a rider on his way to hell and of the horse who carried him there."

War Bride

WAR BRIDE was a three-year-old thoroughbred filly I had the privilege of schooling a number of years ago. She wasn't a conformation horse by a long shot. But Man O'War blood ran in her veins and she possessed a great talent for jumping. I was bringing her along slowly because, after all, she was only a baby and, even though there was a great deal of go in her, I asked her to do only that for which I thought she was ready. I was making an athlete out of her—teaching her to use her talents with the utmost confidence in herself and her rider. But teaching is a two-way street and one bitterly cold night in February, War Bride taught me a lesson which I believe has helped me surmount the more formidable personal obstacles I have encountered since.

The boarding stable was closed for the night. The mare and I were the only ones in the large indoor ring. After a thirty-minute slow workout, I dismounted and set up a single low white gate in the center of the ring. The filly had already jumped a brush fence and wooden coop so, on this particular evening, I felt she was ready for the gate. I remounted and walked her up to it—let her stand for a moment to take a good look, then backed three or four strides and sent her forward.

This was the way we always approached a new obstacle—first we looked, then we jumped. I had never varied this procedure from the very beginning and, until this moment, it had always worked. But tonight it didn't. Tonight War Bride put on her brakes and quit cold. I wasn't too disturbed at first, perhaps her own shadow, cast by the overhead lights had momentarily frightened her or maybe she was just being stubborn. I tried again and she quit again. Now I held her steady in front of the gate with her chest pressing against it, and slapped her lightly across the flank with my open hand. I swung her away, then pivoted sharply and came in again. This time, she stopped and shied off to the left.

After that bad beginning, I tried everything I knew to get her over that gate. I dismounted and set up wings—wooden frames on both sides of the jump—two deep, then four, until they become a long chute with that single white gate at the end. But War Bride continued to run out, taking wings and all with her, smashing timber, almost falling on her face. The situation was rapidly getting out of hand. I began "clashing controls," asking her to go and stop at the same time, confusing the poor horse, causing her to rear and buck and plunge about like a rodeo bronc. She dropped me on the ground three or four times, but after each fall I managed to corner her and climb painfully back into the saddle. She had lost confidence in me, but, by the same token, I was rapidly losing mine in her. It was an even exchange, but a vicious circular one, for, in imperceptible ways, I was telegraphing my loss of heart and robbing her of hers.

The temperature in the ring hovered around twenty degrees, but minutes after we started for that white gate the mare was dripping wet and I could feel my shirt plastered against my back. I wanted to call it off—chicken out. No one was in the building and no one would ever know. But I would—and so would War Bride. Over the following weeks the problem would grow worse. Our mutual trust would be shattered and all of our painstaking work together would be completely wasted. And this horse might never reach the heights for which I felt she was destined.

I had visions of myself, thrown and badly hurt, lying in that ice-cold arena with no one around to help. I tried desperately to control my rising panic and the mad desire to strike back at War Bride's stubbornness. But long ago, I had learned from experience that to inflict pain

can only bring on "blindness" and ultimate disaster.

A wise old horseman once said to me, "When training a horse, never start anything you can't finish." These words flashed into my mind while I balanced on the brink of indecision. And as their meaning sank in, my course became simple and one-way. War Bride was capable of jumping that gate. She was ready and I knew it. So there was nothing left for me to do but pull together whatever courage I had left and finish what I had started. We battled at that crossing for what seemed like an eternity. Neither one of us would back down. I took a number of breaks to catch my breath and let the mare catch hers. I'd let her walk slowly around the ring for several minutes while I slumped exhausted in the saddle, then we'd start all over again.

Finally, almost two hours after we began, War Bride gave up and jumped the gate. Why? I think because I outlasted her—that's all. I was more determined than she was. Then she jumped it again. Confidence came pouring back into me. I removed the wings and sent her over the gate without them. In the last and final test, as we cantered toward the gate, thirty yards away, I dropped the reins on her neck. The lesson was well learned, for she stayed on course and jumped that obstacle as if she had been doing it every day of her life. Right then and there, she learned that she was pointed at a fence for only one reason—to jump it! I believe it was a turning point in her career, for she never quit with me again.

There will always be a warm place in my heart for War Bride. She lived up to all my expectations, winning many working hunter championships in major horse shows and eventually going on to become one of the great horses on the United States Equestrian Team.

Pablita

*N*OT long ago, I read in a newspaper that, in a small village in the northwestern part of Spain, near the Pass of Pancorbo, there was a celebration being held for a horse. I thought perhaps a locally owned steed had won some big race, but when I checked into the matter, I found that the guest of honor was an old dapple gray mare named Pablita, a cart horse.

Why would a whole town give a fiesta for an old draft horse? Well, let me tell you her story, and you can judge for yourself whether the honor was merited.

For years, this little mare pulled a cart filled with fruits and vegetables between two villages which lay in the Asturias, a rugged mountain chain of jagged peaks and rock towers. Every morning, her master drove her to the local market and loaded up. Then he peddled his produce in both villages—one in the morning, and one in the afternoon. The pair would amble slowly through the narrow winding streets. The peddler led the way. His cheerful call, "Apples, peaches, tomatoes," was familiar to all, and everyone admired his gray mare who followed him faithfully, pulling the cartful of fruits and vegetables. She waited as he chatted

with a customer then dogged along behind him when he moved on to the next. This was their routine. Pablita knew her job and did it well—and not once in many years together did she question her master's judgment.

Now, between the two villages, there was a tall boulder-strewn mountain. Some years before, a tunnel had been constructed through it. There was a steep trail over the top, but, since the tunnel had been put through, all the traffic chose the much easier route. From morning until night, automobiles, wagons, trucks, bicycles, carts—everything went through this tunnel.

Late in the morning of July 2, 1968, old Pablita was on the road as usual. Her master drowsed on the high wooden seat behind her. He had had a good morning and now he catnapped as the wagon creaked along. Soon they would be in the next village and, if business was as

PABLITA

good there, he would get home early. He was smiling at the thought, when, without warning, the cart came to a halt. He sat up, jolted into sharp wakefulness. Why had his horse stopped close to the entrance of the tunnel? He could see no obstruction. He slapped the reins across Pablita's back and clucked to her. "Come on, little girl, we haven't got all day," he urged. She moved forward a couple of steps, then stopped again. This time, she swung her head around and eyed her master. "Are you sure you want me to go on?" she seemed to be asking. The peddler was perplexed. He climbed down from the wagon and walked around her, picking up each foot and examining it closely. Maybe a stone was lodged in a hoof . . . but there was no sign of any. He climbed back into the wagon. He picked up the reins and tapped the mare with his whip. She trotted ahead a few paces, but when she reached the entrance of the tunnel, Pablita stopped dead. There was no hesitation in her now. She had made up her mind—this was as far as she was going. Her master got down again, caught hold of her bridle and tried pulling her forward—

but Pablita was not going anywhere. Her legs were planted like four posts. He tugged and jerked and berated her. Behind them, the traffic quickly piled up. There was much yelling and blowing of horns, but the gray mare would not be moved. The tunnel was narrow and the vehicles that went through it alternated in clumps. A signal flag, carried by the last member of one group and handed to the last member of the group going in the opposite direction kept the traffic in motion. Now the horse and cart blocked the entrance so effectively that nothing on wheels could get by. Someone ran through to the other side, about two hundred yards or so, to explain the situation, for it was impossible for anything to turn around, once it was inside the tunnel.

The peddler was really a gentle man, but, because of the pressure behind, he was forced to use his whip. Still the mare would not budge.

A policeman came riding up on his motorcycle. When he was told about the problem, he quickly took over. "Let's get some volunteers," he ordered. "You, you, you!" He assembled six or eight men around the mare and, together they tried to lift her off the ground. She didn't fight them, but her feet seemed to have taken root.

"Unhook the wagon," someone cried.

The peddler unhitched the wagon and it was rolled off to the side of the road. Pablita was still anchored in place. The men gathered around her again, took hold of the leather harness trailing down her sides and began pulling. Pablita sat back on her haunches, braced for battle. As a tug of war commenced, suddenly, above the grunts of the men, a strange vibration could be felt. Everyone stopped in his tracks. Now there was an eerie stillness in the air, almost as if the day were holding its breath. While the men stood alerted, the distant vibration began again, but, this time, it rapidly grew stronger and stronger. The earth trembled beneath their feet, then, right before their very eyes, the inside of the tunnel seemed to explode with a giant roar. The collapsing roof sent great clouds of dust swirling out of both ends of the tunnel—quickly enveloping the horse and men and the scores of people and vehicles lined up behind them. The pounding continued. It rolled and boomed, then gradually subsided to a rumble, like distant thunder. As the dust settled, the gray mare and the men gathered around her could be seen still standing there, shocked but alive. And in front of them the

PABLITA

face of the mountain swept upwards, unbroken, with no sign of the tunnel anywhere.

Did Pablita know that cave-in was coming? I'm sure she did. It was this awareness, this sixth-sense of impending danger and her refusal to enter the tunnel that saved the lives of so many.

Can you think of a better reason for a celebration in honor of a horse?

The Story of Sleepy Tom

SLEEPY TOM was born in the late 1860's, in a brush pile behind a little red schoolhouse, in the State of Ohio. His dam was Old Wetchie, a mare owned by a tavern keeper, Pop Dingler. He was a scrawny, sickly little thing, but the two small Dingler boys couldn't have been more pleased. Their dad had promised them this foal, so the worse he looked, the better were their chances of getting him. The colt was so weak he could hardly support his own weight. As a result, he slept continuously. Any time anyone walked into the pasture, he might have seen the feeble creature lying off by himself—lost to the world. It wasn't long before he became known as "that Sleepy Tom foal." The boys had to hold him up to his mother while he nursed and they took turns massaging the spindly legs, trying to promote the circulation in them. Pop Dingler would have destroyed the little fellow, but the one thing that delayed this harsh decision was the fact that the mare had such excellent bloodlines, and the sire was the well-known Tom Rolfe, who in turn was by a famed racing champion Pocahontas.

As time went on, with the help of the two Dingler boys, the colt steadily grew bigger and stronger. Blood will tell and by the time

Sleepy Tom was three years old, he began showing signs of the racing blood that coursed through his veins.

One day, Pop Dingler saw Tom pace across the field—coming in for his evening grain. So impressed was he by the youngster's dazzling speed that, at the supper table that night, he informed his boys that he was taking over the colt's future education. And it wasn't long before Tom became involved with all sorts of "nag racing." Dingler was determined to get the most out of this young horse, but he was completely unconcerned with his welfare. All that mattered to him and his cronies was the fast dollar and as long as Tom kept winning, he would be fed and cared for.

But you can't win 'em all and, in time, Tom lost more and more races. He would go lame periodically from the constant abuse to his

young legs and, eventually, he broke down. To add to his problem, a milky film appeared on his eyes and, at this point, it looked as if his racing days were coming to an end.

Meanwhile, trainer, Steve Phillips, at the far end of the State of Ohio, heard about Tom's racing ability and set out to see if he could buy him. But when he got to the tavern, he found that Dingler had gotten rid of the horse about two months previously. Steve Phillips did not give up and for almost a year, he tried to track down Sleepy Tom.

One afternoon, a friend passing through Steve's home village informed the trainer that he believed he had seen Tom tied to a hitching post outside of a saloon in a neighboring town. Steve dropped what he was doing and left immediately to follow this new lead. Sure enough, it was Sleepy Tom. He had become stone blind and, even though he was only six, an age when some horses are just reaching maturity, Tom looked like an old nag. His head hung so low, his droopy lower lip brushed the ground. He was awfully thin too, and his feet were split and broken by the hard roads he had been driven over. Inside the saloon, his owner sagged across a corner table—his bleary, bloodshot eyes contemplating the empty whiskey bottle in front of him. Seven dollars and a fresh bottle closed the deal and, five minutes later, Tom went limping down the road, hitched to the back of Steve Phillips' buggy.

The trainer's first move was to build Tom up again. This takes a long time when a horse is badly run down because the process begins on the inside and works outward. But plenty of good hay, grain and water and a relaxed routine which never varied, slowly brought the horse around to his normal self. The blindness was irreparable. To overcome this, Steve had to establish a mutual confidence between himself and the horse. Just as a blind man learns to rely completely on his guide dog, so Tom came to depend upon Steve. The trainer never gave the horse a "bum steer." Soon, Tom could be driven in harness at a walk, and before long was ready to race again.

Tom didn't make his comeback as just an ordinary racer. He was a champion, with the heart of a champion, and he went out and proved what he was really made of.

Thousands flocked to the tracks to see the blind horse beat the best pacers of that time. Tom's greatest day was in 1879, when he won the fifth heat of a special event in Chicago. He showed his heels to the top pacers in the record time (for that era) of 2:12¼.

Not long afterwards, during a difficult financial setback, Steve Phillips was forced to sell his horse. Old Tom went on valiantly, nevertheless, and, under his new owner, continued his winning ways.

The glitter and victories eventually vanished, however, and, once again, Tom was sold—this time to a carriage painter.

Several years passed. Steve Phillips thought many times about the horse he had helped come back. Often he berated himself for having let Tom go. He was continuously plagued by guilt and a sickening sense of having betrayed a friend. Finally, he decided he must get Tom back. The old horse must spend his last days with him. Through inquiry, he learned that Tom was in a livery stable in Bear Creek County. Steve drove for two days and reached there as the sun was going down. But he had arrived too late. The night before, a fire had swept through the stables and now all that was left were the charred ruins—still smoldering red in the waning light.

All this happened nearly a century ago. Since then, many good horses have come and gone, but no roster perpetuating the great horses of history would be complete without the name of Sleepy Tom.

The River

*I*T WAS the last year my family lived in the house on Lincoln Street, in Wilkes-Barre, Pennsylvania, which means I must have been around twelve or thirteen years old. I've often thought about this incident and how, through ignorance and over-vidid imaginations we can sometimes churn up a whole lot of unnecessary trouble.

My most constant companion at that time, was Phil Cutler. I lived near the Lackawanna railroad tracks—as a matter of fact, right alongside of them. I could get to Phil's in a few minutes by following the rails for about a half mile, then cutting across the lumber yard to his house on the south end of town. During my summer vacation, I made this trip about twice a day. I actually didn't care much for Phil. He was fat, with small pig eyes and a crazy unpredictable temper from which I always backed off. I could have licked him easily, but I adored his father's horse Bonny and didn't want to take any chances of losing her.

Mr. Cutler was a vegetable peddler. Each morning of the week, he loaded his wagon with produce and, with Bonny hitched up front, looking very elegant and efficient in her brass-trimmed leather harness, they'd be gone for the day. Occasionally, I would meet them in the

streets of Wilkes-Barre and would never fail to stop and chat with "my horse." I suppose now I'd see all kinds of things wrong with her, but at that time, I figured she was just about the most beautiful horse in the world. Her coat was dark brown, almost black, and there was a thin white stripe running down the middle of her face. Her eyes always seemed pensive, as if she were constantly remembering some far-off wonderful place. I'd press my cheek against her muzzle, just to feel her warm breath, rich with the aroma of hay and oats, and I don't know what else—but it always smelled sweet and was somehow terribly exciting.

I remember the greatest thing about the whole week was Sunday, when Mr. Cutler allowed Phil and me to take Bonny out for the afternoon. I lived for this day. We rode her bareback, Phil up front and me behind him, with my arms wrapped around his expansive waist. Mounted in this manner, Bonny walked down East Northampton Street, through town, then across the Market Street bridge to Kirby Park, on the other side of the Susquehanna River.

There, Phil and I would take turns riding around the bridle paths. I would make believe I was the movie cowboy, Gary Cooper, thundering across the plains with Indians in hot pursuit. Lying flat along my pony's neck, I'd turn and fire, again and again. Up ahead was the stockade—could I make it? It was great fun, this make-believe, especially since I was riding a real live horse.

It was during one of these daydreaming rides that the thought first hit me—what if I came to a river? The Indians were closing fast. I had seen this happen to Gary Cooper once—but it didn't stop him. His horse, without hesitation, dove into the river. He surfaced and swam strongly with Cooper hanging onto the pommel of his saddle. The Indians fired after them. Bullets plunked all around, but they reached the far shore unscathed and got safely away.

I was sure Bonny and I could pull off the same escape. I told my plan to Phil. But suppose Bonny had never been in the water in her life? Well, that could be remedied very easily. We would condition her for the big swim!

All through the following week, when she returned from work, we hosed Bonny down. Mr. Cutler had no objections. After all, this was the middle of a long hot summer. It would do the old mare a lot of good. If he had known what we were planning for her, he'd have slapped us

THE RIVER

both in chains—and maybe it would have been a good idea if he had.

The next Sunday afternoon finally came, sunny and hot. So far so good. When Phil, Bonny and I reached the far side of the Market Street bridge, instead of turning left into the park, we went right, up river along the shore, headed toward the North Street bridge. As Phil and I sat our horse there, looking out across the black swirling waters of the Susquehanna, my heart began sinking rapidly. I could see Phil's had already reached bottom, but Bonny looked very alert and unperturbed. Her head was up as she sniffed the coal fumes which rose from the water. She wouldn't have been so calm if she knew what was in store for her.

"You go first," said Phil.

"No, you go. It's your horse."

"But it was your idea," he parried.

I couldn't deny that.

"Okay," I retorted, "if that's the way you want it."

I was getting angry now, mostly because I was so scared. Phil slid off and there I was up front, alone, with only Bonny's head between me and the river. It was now or never. With a wild cowboy yell, I dug my heels into her sides. Instinctively, she lunged forward. Loose shale rolling under her feet sent her down the bank at an alarming rate of speed. I'm sure she would have stopped at the water's edge, but her own momentum, plus the crumbling bank, carried us over the brink. The cold waters enveloped us and I was instantly separated from my mount. It was pitch dark. I could feel Bonny all around me and I kept clutching at her, but it was like trying to catch hold of an eel. Suddenly, we broke surface, under the bridge, where the waters rushed through in a powerful whirlpool, and we were both sucked right into the middle of it. Against the bright sky, I could see Bonny's head as she struggled to stay afloat. Her ears were flat back and her mouth was wide open. I was underneath her neck, holding on for dear life, but she was slipping away fast. I let go and tried for her mane, then slid down along her back. What a toboggan ride! I came off her hindquarters feet first, still trying to grab anything, and at that instant, my fingers locked into her tail.

We were now heading downstream, toward the Market Street bridge, almost a mile away. I could see Phil running along the shore, trying to keep up, but we were rapidly outdistancing him. Bonny and I

were perhaps seventy-five yards off shore and all I wanted now was to get back on land. The Indians could have me for all I cared. They couldn't frighten me any more than I was right now. But the situation seemed hopeless. After the Market Street bridge, the river widened and deepened, and judging by the direction in which the current was taking us, it would be impossible to reach shore. Bonny was blowing like a whale. Spray spouted from her nostrils. Occasionally, her front legs would surface like a giant thrashing machine, then they would suddenly lose power and we'd go under, rolling crazily, to rise again for a fraction of a minute before the waters closed over us once more. Each time we came up, I sucked in as much air as I could. Now half of the intake was water. I began gagging and choking. My head was bursting and my lungs were burning up. I think perhaps, at this moment, I felt I had been betrayed by Gary Cooper and all the rest of the cowboys and Indians who had gotten me into this mess.

A jolt shot through Bonny, as if she had struck bottom. A submerged sand bar stretched out into the river from the shore and it was this bar that Bonny and I slammed up against. In frantic, desperate lunges, belly deep, the mare made her way to shore. I let go of her tail and followed as best I could, gasping for air all the way. At the bank, I collapsed and began wretching into the earth. Bonny stood over me. I could hear the wind whistling through her lungs. Her heaving sides rocked her back and forth so hard I thought she might fall down right on top of me, but I was too weak to move out of her way.

THE RIVER

Phil came running down to us. "I thought you were both goners," he yelled in my ear.

It was dark by the time we reached home. Bonny was still covered with black river silt, but, behind the barn, we washed her down with soap and water. She seemed tired but, happily, none the worse for her wild experience.

I thought this was the end of the cowboy incident, but, a few months later, Phil and I were sitting on their kitchen porch when Mr. Cutler came home. We heard him say to his wife, "I don't know what's got into that horse. Today, in the middle of South Main Street, she wouldn't go through a puddle of water. I never saw her like this. We held up traffic for more than ten minutes. Finally, I had to get down and lead her to the other side of the street and around the water. It was absolutely crazy."

Phil and I stared at each other, speechless with the knowledge of what we had done. Bonny would never go through water again. Mr. Cutler tried everything he knew to overcome this phobia, but the brown mare would have no part of it. Finally, in exasperation, he sold "my horse" and, a short time later, bought a motor truck to replace her.

Even now, many years later, I still get a warm glow whenever I think of Bonny. But, it is always followed by the sad realization that I had no one to blame for her loss but myself.

Midnight

THE horse has had a full time job ever since man discovered that he could slap a saddle on him and ride, or hitch him to a wagon and drive him.

He has charged into battle to the din of clashing steel, and dragged caissons through murderous shellfire. He has pulled a stagecoach over seemingly impassable mountain trails, and carried the United States mail. He has also achieved moments of fame by winning a Kentucky Derby or a Grand National, and shared the spotlight with such famous movie cowboys as Gene Autry and Roy Rogers. But, in spite of his varied duties and changing roles, the horse has remained the servant, man the master. Most horses accept this readily and happily.

However, there is one kind of horse that has reversed this scheme of things—the bucking bronco, rodeo's glorious misfit! His ancestry may combine the blood of ponderous Clydesdales and bony, snake-eyed Indian Mustangs, neat little Texas bred cow ponies, with maybe a strain of Shetland Pony or Thoroughbred stallion thrown in for good measure. As a type, the bronco emerged late in the nineteenth century, when farm horses were brought to the unfenced ranges of the West, and some

strange mismatches were made—mostly at the discretion of the horses. The bucker's manners are very bad, his disposition is worse, and he doesn't go for this "horse is man's faithful servant" business. He believes man's place is on the ground and he has dedicated his life to keeping him there.

The rodeo world has known many outstanding buckers—Steamboat, Broken Box, Crying Squaw, Tumbleweed, Hell's Angel, and the indomitable Midnight.

Even today, Midnight's bronc career is remembered as one of the greatest in rodeo history. He was foaled in 1915, in Southern Alberta, Canada. As a three-year-old, he was a good working cowhorse, but at four, when he came in from winter range, his working days on the ranch were over. I suppose no one will ever know what changed his attitude, but from that time until the end of his fourteen-year rodeo

MIDNIGHT

career, nobody rode on Midnight for the qualifying time of ten seconds. That's quite a record, isn't it?

Pete Knight, one of the top rodeo riders of all time, was Midnight's most persistent challenger. Pete risked his neck aboard the black tornado in rodeos at Vancouver, Pendleton, Columbus, Fort Worth, and Cheyenne. At Cheyenne in 1934, for seven of the longest seconds in Rodeo, Pete tried to keep himself in the middle of that bronc. He was determined to stay the whole way, but Midnight was the best bucker in the business and he proved it that memorable afternoon. It took just six seconds to loosen his rider. In the seventh, he executed a terrific straight up and down buck followed by a shoulder whip that sent Pete into the dust.

Following the 1939 Cheyenne Frontier Days Rodeo, Midnight was retired from competition, still undefeated, still champion. He was turned out to pasture on the Johnstown, Colorado, ranch of Verne Elliot, the rodeo producer who owned him. For two years, Midnight lived there with two other retired veterans and his endless memories of a glorious past. Nobody ever put a saddle on him again, but on November fifth, 1936, death quietly rode him out.

Colorado Senator Chris Cusack wrote the epitaph on his gravestone, and if ever you're driving through that part of the country, you might stop by and read it.

>Underneath this sod lies a great
>   bucking hoss.
>There never lived a cowboy he
>   couldn't toss.
>His name was Midnight, his coat
>   black as coal.
>If there's a hoss Heaven, Please
>   God rest his soul.

Moifaa

ONE of the most inspiring horse stories I have heard in recent years concerns a New Zealand thoroughbred named Moifaa.

He was a big brown rangy colt of depth and substance, and, even though he won many races in his native country, his appearance always prompted hoots of laughter from the crowd and comments such as, "He looks like a starved elephant," or "What do you call that thing?"

True enough, Moifaa was not a handsome horse. He was not only awkward and ungainly-looking, but he stood over seventeen hands high. Now, a horse that large, especially a race horse, is usually not as well coordinated or as athletic as the more average sixteen-hand horse. But Moifaa's owner, wealthy pioneer Spencer Golland, had great faith in his horse's capabilities. One year he decided to send the animal to England, to run in the Grand National, which is the most famous steeplechase race in the world—and the most demanding. The course is four miles long and the thirty fences are big and solid. As many as forty horses will start in this race, but perhaps only seven or eight will finish. The casualties are high and a Grand National steeplechaser must be a good bold jumper. He must also have a lot of class, speed and staying

power. Otherwise, he won't have a chance of getting around, much less winning a truly run National. Outside of his looks, Moifaa seemed to have these qualifications, but how much more he had is what this story is about.

The colt was shipped to England several months before the time set for the running of the big race, so that he would have plenty of time for conditioning. Off Capetown, South Africa, the freighter that was carrying Moifaa ran into a terrific storm. For two days it buffeted the small vessel. The cargo in the hold broke free, slamming up against the bulkhead. The ship wallowed and began to split apart. The crew frantically lowered lifeboats and the passengers were taken to safety. Moifaa, however, still locked in his special stall which had been erected on the deck, was left to his fate. As the seas rose and closed in, the trapped horse must have decided it was time to leave. He methodically kicked his way out of the stall and leaped over the side of the doomed freighter, going along with everything else that wasn't tied down.

Once in the water, he instinctively swam for his life. Twenty-foot waves washed over him, then lifted and flung him about with herculean force. Moifaa was under water more than above, but he wouldn't give up—I suppose because he just didn't know how. There was no panic in him, just the will to reach land. How this horse survived is absolutely incredible. He was in the water for hours and finally staggered up on the lonely rocky beach of a small island, almost a hundred miles from where the ship had gone down.

Can you imagine what that hundred miles must have been like? I don't think a human could have done it—his own realization of the hopelessness of the situation would have drained the fight clean out of him. But a horse knows nothing of such things. His will to live is "right now," and what lies ahead plays no part in his makeup. Now Moifaa lay at the water's edge, his heaving sides bruised and bleeding from the awful beating he had taken—but he was alive.

He stayed where he was all night, too exhausted to move, but by morning, gnawing hunger pains sent him wandering along the shore, foraging for whatever he could find. And there wasn't enough to feed a rabbit. He turned inland, over the dunes, and soon came across marsh grass that grew in clumps and tasted quite salty. Afterwards, he found water to drink in the many stagnant pools that had collected in pockets

between the sparse vegetation.

Moifaa lived this way for several months. He grew thin and his coat lost much of its luster, but his constant search for food kept him on his feet.

He wandered around and around the small island. Occasionally, he ventured into the center of the rocky terrain, but he always came back to the shore, to stand and stare out across the endless sea. He had never known such loneliness in his life. Perhaps as he stood there, he remembered when he wasn't hungry all the time—and people fussed over him—and crowds cheered when he raced to victory.

A fisherman was coming in with his catch one evening. Suddenly, he thought he saw a movement on the shore of a small island he was sailing past. The sun had already gone down and the visibility wasn't too good. He peered through the mist at the island he'd thought was uninhabited. But what was that standing near the shore? It might be a deer but, by gosh, it looked a heck of a lot like a horse!

He turned his boat and headed toward the shore. Moifaa had been nibbling on some dry weeds. He raised his head and watched the sailboat approach. Then the fisherman called and Moifaa answered with a shrill whinny and came galloping down to meet his rescuer.

That's the way he was found. The proper authorities were notified and, after the rescue operations were completed, Moifaa resumed his interrupted journey to England. He arrived shortly before the Grand National.

Spencer Golland was there to meet the horse and quickly took over his reconditioning. The day for the running of the great race arrived. The foremost horse racing enthusiasts in the world were there, (including King Edward VII, whose own horse also was racing). The New Zealand colt had still not regained his top form but the game look in his eyes were there and the heart.

Golland said, "I've seen him in better shape, but this is what he came for, so let's let him run."

Well, Moifaa raced in that Grand National of 1904—and won it by eight lengths. To make the "fairy tale ending" even better, he was subsequently purchased by the Prince of Wales and lived happily ever after in royal splendor.